Table Of Co

Who You Really Are!

There is a lot more to you than your physical body. You may have heard the cliché,

"You are a spiritual being having a physical experience."

That's what you are, a spiritual being. You, the being, are more than the body that you have today. That means there is more to you than a physical shell. Look into a mirror and look beyond your physical reflection. Look deeply into your eyes; really look and you will see the truth.

The physical body that you inhabit has a limited existence. It will die. You, the real you, the spiritual being that I am talking about, will continue and live forever.

When I say you, I mean your essence. You might call this your soul or your spirit. The real you can be found behind the personality that you display to the world. The real you is not your personality. You are a non-physical entity, a consciousness that is eternal. You are a being of light that vibrates at a certain frequency. Your existence is not limited to the time constraints of this one lifetime. The real you lives longer than the physical you. The real you is the individual that stands out from the crowd when it is allowed full expression. Your essence takes this individuality along for the ride from one physical existence to the next.

The essence that is you occupies your physical body for a purpose rather than at random chance. I mean your physical body as distinct from anyone else's physical body. Perhaps you have already asked yourself why you have your body. Why you are tall or short, why you were born in America, Australia or any other place.

This is a deliberate act on your part. The real you decided on this life and your current circumstances. It was your choice.

When you die your essence continues. The physical body that you picked and inhabit right now eventually ceases to exist.

Your personality belongs to this physical body and the circumstances you have now. Your personality is left behind as you leave your body behind. Your personality is your mask and it has certain traits that you have inherited and traits that you have developed throughout your life.

Your personality is what you display on the outside. Some people are extroverts; their outgoing nature endears them in all sorts of social situations. Other people are serious by nature and keep to themselves. The combinations of personality traits are endless, as are the occupations and hobbies that people gravitate towards.

Your mask of personality is a cover for the real you. It protects you from a perceived enemy called life. That's why you hide. You believe that it is safer behind your mask.

We Are All One

"The journey of a thousand miles begins with one step."

Lao Tzu

The answer is only one.

We are all one and the same, parts of the whole. Let me explain this further. That means that you and I are one and the same. We are made from the same stuff. You and I and everyone else, including the bad guys, are all a part of the all-encompassing energy source that is the universe. It's not just you and me; it's every living thing and also every non-living thing. We are all a part of the creator; some people call it the source. Let me give the source another term, which many people are scared of: God.

Note: God is not meant as a religious term. The God you are reading about is the God that covers everything and everyone, irrespective of their religion, color or political beliefs. Yes, the bad guys are covered here as well. It doesn't matter what you call it, him or her, as long as you understand what I am talking about.

Everything is energy. The energy is alive and all encompassing. The source or the creator is like one giant bundle of intelligent energy. You are part of it.

This is a very important point. The energy is present because it is you. This is an unchangeable fact. You can either take charge of it or be swept along in its wake. You will discover more about this in later chapters.

Because you and I and everyone else are all one, whatever you do affects everything else. This is in proportion, of course, to the magnitude and energy behind what you do. That means if you have a negative thought it will not bring down the world, however it will affect the people around you. Have you ever worked in an environment where there is a negative person? What happens to the atmosphere of your work place? The answer is: it deteriorates.

Your body, the chair you are sitting on and the roof that you shelter under are all made from the energy that makes up the universe. This energy is one giant malleable substance that is shaped and rearranged to appear as everything you see. All of this is temporary.

Sometimes you don't see that you are one with everything else because of three reasons:

1. The whole is too big to see in its entirety. You can only see a small part of the planet earth, yet you are standing on it.

2. You are inside of the whole so your perspective doesn't allow you to see. Look at the difference in what you see when you are inside your house and if you go outside and look at your house. Your house looks completely different.

3. The relationship between cause and effect has a large delay in the physical world. That means everything you do has an effect but there is often a delay so that you don't realize that what you have done has a consequence. This is a deliberate delay and we shall cover it in more detail later.

How You Are Here

There is a good reason we are all contained in different bodies. Read on and let me tell you a story that will help you understand.

God or the all-encompassing energy source is everything and it is one thing. In other words it is the whole. When something is everything and only one thing, it doesn't have a beginning or an end.

Anything that has a beginning or an end cannot be everything. Everything means just that. It means that there is no edge. God is the universe that you live in and there is no end to your universe.

When something is everything or is the whole, when there is nothing else and the whole is everywhere, then logic says that there is nowhere that this 'thing' is not. It's everywhere.

This causes a dilemma because the one concept that would be impossible is that of the self. When there is only one thing and that thing is everything then the concept of its self would be unfamiliar. The concept of yourself can only be understood if there is someone or something to compare you with.

The concept of self is the only thing not experienced by the source. I say not experienced instead of unknown because if the source is everything and is an all-encompassing intelligence, then it would intellectually know of the concept but not be able to experience it.

Separation is a term that is often coined to explain the beginning of all things. The original energy source or God split into two temporarily in order to know its self. Splitting into two allows one part to see the reflection of its self in the other. The split is a reflection because the one thing is actually everything.

When this everything splits into two, it can't divide into a collection of individual pieces and distribute them into different areas. It can't do this because it is a malleable living intelligent energy that is everything. For this split to occur each part will have all the parts that the other has. The result is two different, but very much the same, versions of everything.

This split is a temporary reflection, not a division. Temporary implies time. Relative to the size of the whole this happens instantaneously. To us, however, it appears as time, eons of time. How much time is an eon? Answer: a long time, longer than you and I can count.

When there are two there is actually a third. This happens because there is a void where the two are not.

Originally there was one, which means there is no void because the one is everywhere and there is nowhere that it isn't. When there is no void you can't have two because it becomes one.

When there are two it means that there are really three:

1. The first of the two.

2. The second of the two.

3. The space between the two.

It gets better. The one is everything and because of this it can't be two things and a third which is nothing.

If this were the case then it would not be everything, as we understand it. So what happens is that the reflections after separating return to the whole. They instantaneously relative to the source become whole again.

This sounds simple except for one complicating factor that we haven't yet covered.

Once the first split occurs and there are two, a cycle has begun. It's a cycle that continues forever as far as we are concerned. From the perspective of the two parts, each needs to split into two in order for it to understand the concept of self. This occurs because each of the two that originally split is actually one all-encompassing everything and therefore still cannot know itself.

It needs to split into two and reflect itself.

The process starts again with each of the parts splitting into two, reflecting and merging again. The cycle that now occurs continues forever, each split causing its fragments to get smaller and smaller.

Stand in front of a mirror with another mirror behind you. What do you see? The reflections of light continue forever.

You are this process on a smaller scale. You are one of the splits in the process of rejoining the whole. In order for you to find the whole again, you need to travel through the void that was created in the split. The further away you are from the source or the light, the darker it is. Here in the physical world you are a long way from the source. You are traveling through the void and returning home. This is a journey that will take many lifetimes, as you know it. **For your creator**, which you are a part of, this occurs in an instant. Life as we know it is for the creator the rejoining in an instant to the source. You are reflecting this on a much smaller scale. It's like when you breathe in and then out, except on a much larger scale. The scope of this act is beyond your comprehension. When you are in this physical form you only see the part that you live, and because you are inside the whole, your perspective is distorted.

The void is where God or the all-encompassing energy is not present. God is light and where there is no light there is darkness.

Darkness is not a thing as such, it is the absence of something, and that something is light. God is also love, and so evil, which is the absence of love, does not actually exist. Evil is only the absence of love.

The void or the darkness is a temporary aberration on the larger scale of the whole. It happens in an instant and then is gone.

Your perspective is different; you see this through the concept of time and living your life because:

1. The vast difference in size between you and the whole.

2. The distance of your split from the whole. You are a small and distant fragment.

Time is an illusion. We are actually moving through the energy back to the source. The source is everything. It is everything therefore everything already exists. That means that every eventuality or possibility already exists.

You are moving through the space of the energy that is everything. You don't see that you move because of the vast size of the whole, just like you don't see that the earth moves, even though you are standing on it everyday. If you use your eyes to look at the sun it appears to move in the sky. Mathematics and astronomy have shown that the earth is actually moving.

You move through space, which is every possibility and eventuality. I don't mean space, the dark place without atmosphere that the space shuttle zooms around in. That is the space between the planets. The space that you move through can't be measured in this way, nonetheless it exists because you are in it.

This book is concerned with showing you the techniques to get what you want. That means you are learning to dial into the location or frequency of where you want to be. It already exists, that's why with your mind you can get whatever you want. The hard part is finding out where in space it is and turning the dial. When you want to get what you want you are actually going to a location. You can go anywhere you wish. You can choose.

God or the all-encompassing source is love and light. Where God is not, you are left with a void or darkness. Light and darkness are opposites. Opposites exist in order to know the range of experience that defines what you are studying. Opposites create contrast and this allows you to experience. The concept of duality is the concept of contrasting opposites. When the all-encompassing source splits in order to reflect itself you have duality. This happens because you have an opposite to the all-encompassing everything, which is the void. The void is nothing.

Opposites are really the same, just at a different location on a sliding scale of an experience.

Without each of the opposites we could not experience the other. For us to know one thing we must experience the concept of its shifting range and opposite pole. In order for you to experience the feeling of being full after a meal, you had to experience being hungry first. If you have never felt hunger then you cannot know the feeling of being full.

The concept of duality also appears in you. Inside of you are two opposites. Let's call them your Lower Self and your Higher Self. Your Higher Self is the real you. Some people call your Higher Self your Super Consciousness or your Creative Consciousness; others refer to it as your Over Soul.

This is the part of you that is love.

Your Lower Self is also known as your Ego and is the part of you that resides in fear. Fear is the opposite of love. Love is the energy that binds the universe.

Your Lower Self is the vacuum that is created when your Higher Self is not present. This allows undesirable or negative energy, amongst other things, to dominate your consciousness. Both your Higher Self and your Lower Self are different poles of the same state, which is consciousness. The duality in you is actually an illusion. The illusion exists in order for you to see yourself. It is your job to find the balance point between the poles so that the illusion of duality disappears. The balance point is the mid-point between poles, and this actually allows for the light of God or the source to shine through.

Achieving the balance point between opposite poles means that you have removed the emotional pull that occurs from each of the poles. It is emotion that pulls us to one side. Without emotion you have preferences instead of the more extreme likes and dislikes that you create. You will learn more about this in later chapters.

You can start to remove the concept of duality from your life by doing two things:

1.   Changing your inner self, eliminating needs and desires and changing them to preferences.

2.   You can also look at life with a different perspective.
      • Look at a person instead of a male or a female.

      • Look at people instead of blacks and whites.

      • Look at life instead of plants, animals and people.

• View our planet as one instead of looking at the different countries.

• Have preferences instead of strong emotional pulls. Look at both sides of the argument.

How The Life Works

"Our prime purpose in this life is to help others. And if you can't help them, at least don't hurt them."

Dalai Lama

You already know that everything is energy. Everything that you see around you is made of energy. It is the energy of light. It makes up the molecules that comprise your world. The clothes you wear, the ground you are standing on and the building you are sheltered in are all made from this energy.

Your thoughts are energy and a collection of thoughts in one direction holds more energy than a single thought. Your emotions are also energy. This energy is everywhere and extends beyond the earth and to the end of the universe.

You are also energy. You are energy that vibrates to a certain frequency. Every part of you and your body is energy. There is more to you than you can currently see. You have your own energy field that surrounds you, extends in the space around you beyond your physical body and goes with you wherever you are.

You exist in a stream of energy that connects you to the universe. You have a mind that interprets the energy around you. The interpretation of this energy is subjective. It depends entirely on who you are. You interpret and influence the energy that flows through you depending on the state of the energy that is you. In other words, the purer you are in terms of energy the less you will distort the energy that flows through you.

Energy is permanent and cannot be destroyed, it can only be changed and reshaped. This is one of the basic laws of physics. That's why when you, the energy that is you, leaves your physical body you only reappear somewhere else. The energy that is the real you is never lost or destroyed.

The same applies to the thoughts you put out. Put out means the thoughts that you think. They are also a form of energy, and as such they are permanent. As your thoughts leave you they do not vanish into nothing, they are an energy that remains somewhere as a thought.

All energy vibrates at different frequencies. Frequency is a unit of measurement that is convenient to explain energy with. It is simply the rate at which something vibrates. All energy holds a particular frequency.

Energy that vibrates slowly has a low frequency. You see and experience this type of energy as something dense or solid;

your table, your next-door neighbor or your dog is an example of this. It's easy to see this energy with your eyes or feel it with your hands.

Energy that vibrates quickly has a high frequency. You experience high-frequency energy as something that you cannot see. High frequency energy is not solid. Your thoughts or the energy field that is around you are examples of this. You may be able to feel or intuit this energy. If you have developed certain faculties you may even be able to see this energy when others around you cannot.

Living things have a higher frequency than non-living things. That means your neighbor is vibrating at a higher frequency than your kitchen table.

Energy of the highest frequency is love. You sometimes interpret this energy as white light. Love is the universal energy. The energy of pure love feels like a sweet liquid of light that envelops you and is almost unbearable in its beauty. I say unbearable because the human body can only hold energy up to a certain frequency. Very high frequency energy feels magnificent but is also uncomfortable. It is very difficult for me to describe it to you with words.

As your level of consciousness increases or as you allow more of your Higher Self to shine through, your frequency will increase.

Energy of different frequency is restricted loosely to certain dimensions. Dimensions are just areas that house the different frequencies. Each dimension has a corresponding vibration. You are in the third dimension. Physical life, as you know it, is in the third dimension. What you know as spirit exists in the fourth to seventh dimensions. The energy of the seventh dimension has a higher frequency than that of the third. If you wish to move into the higher dimensions you need to do one or both of the following: increase your vibration or leave your physical body.

Each dimension is subject to different rules of operation. In your third dimension the relationship between cause and effect has a delay. Cause and effect is the relationship of energy or simply what happens when energy is moved. Your thoughts are energy and they have an effect. In the third dimension the effect of your thoughts is subject to a delay before you see the effect. If you move to the next dimension then the relationship between cause and effect is closer. What you think happens a lot sooner after you think it.

Your body has its own energy system. Your body is a sophisticated transmitter and receiver of energy at a variety of frequencies. That means the way you are influences the way the world appears to you.

Energy travels through the human body via a system of interconnected energy points, which are often called chakras. Chakra is a Sanskrit word that means wheel of light. Energy passes through these chakras and ultimately affects you physically depending on how this energy is processed.

There are seven main energy points between the top of your head and the bottom of your spine. They run along the line of your spine. Starting from the top, the chakras are known as:

- o crown
- o third eye
- o throat
- o heart
- o solar plexus
- o sacral
- o base.

The lower three connect you to the earth or things that are of this physical world, and the three highest connect you to your Higher Self.

The clearer your system is, the easier the flow of energy to you and from you. Emotions and other energies can stain, block and distort the flow of energy, and this ultimately affects you physically.

You can easily influence your frequency or vibration. Everything you do, including thinking, has an effect on your energy. You can increase the rate at which your energy vibrates by doing the following:

1. Learning about and dealing with emotion. Emotions cloud your energy field. Emotions stop the real you shining through and allow your personality to remain firmly rooted in the physical world.

2. Eating foods that are fresh and clean. Certain foods are of a higher vibration. Generally fruit and vegetables are in this category. Meats and dairy products and processed foods should be ingested in moderation.

3. Staying away from negative energies. Negative energy sources could be negative people, cigarettes or chemicals, including those found in processed foods.

4. Learning to control your thought patterns to create a state
    of higher vibration. The thoughts you have which come
    from your interpretation of your experiences can be
    positive or they can be negative and in turn influence your
    emotions.

Cause and effect means that every action has an equal
reaction. Any action you perform expends energy and this
energy has to go somewhere. This is another way of saying
that energy cannot be lost, only changed and reshaped.

Whenever there is movement of energy there is also a
disturbing or a changing of the energy of the whole.

It's like you sitting in your bath full of water. When you move to
another position in the bath you disturb the water and any of
the rubber ducks and other toys you have floating around with
you. When you settle in your new position everything
eventually settles. It's all the same; you are there, the water is
there and so is your rubber duck. At the same time it's also
different because everything is in a different position.

All of your actions, thoughts and feelings have a driving
intention. This is a cause and there is always a corresponding
effect somewhere. The law of cause and effect means that
you are responsible for everything that comes from you – this

includes what you think and what you feel – rather than the common misconception that someone or something else is to blame.

The way you interpret energy is the cause and it always has an effect. The world around you is energy. There is a constant stream of energy that continually tries to flow through you. The way you interpret this energy becomes your thoughts. Thoughts are energy in as much as you have reworked the original energy that you come into contact with and shaped it according to your own individual perceptions.

Your thoughts are a cause and they always have a corresponding effect. You don't see this because:

1. You are not aware of what you are thinking.

2. One thought alone doesn't have that much energy associated with it.

3. There is a delay, which is a safety mechanism unique to the third dimension. The delay is in the process of converting thought to matter. It's much easier to see the consequences of your physical actions. This enables you to study the cause and the effect of what you have done.

The law of cause and effect cannot be changed. It is here with you as long as you exist.

We can move one step further to something known as karma. Karma takes the law of cause and effect one step further. Every action actually has an equal and opposite reaction. Every time you do something, it is an action. This action or cause has a reaction or an effect. The effect or reaction has at least an equal amount of energy and it occurs in the opposite direction.

Very simply this means that whatever you send out comes back to you. You may struggle with this concept because you do not directly see the effects of what you put out. Usually if you look carefully and objectively back over your life and reflect on what has happened, you can see the truth of this.

Karma is the way that cause and effect are balanced. Karma is a system for the balancing of the energy that is processed from all living things. It reaches far beyond our physical world. It follows and affects you as you move from one lifetime to the next. That means that sometimes you have created such a ripple in your bath water that the water does not settle for some lifetimes. It happens this way because energy is never lost. As you bend and twist the energy that you come into contact with, there is a system that restores it to its original shape – this is karma.

Karma has nothing to do with morals. It is not about good or bad. It is only a balancing of energy. Good and bad is a subjective judgment that you make. Karma is impersonal.

Physically you experience karma as whatever you give out comes back to you. For every action, there is an equal and opposite reaction. When you give out love then you will get it back from somewhere. If you give out hate then you will get hate back.

Sometimes karma does not settle events immediately. Sometimes the effect of your cause does not come back for an extended period of time. This is especially true for thoughts and feelings. This delay is necessary in your physical world because you are yet to master the process of your thoughts. Without this delay the world would be chaos. You are not yet in control of your own thought process, and as such without the delay effect the world would be in chaos. Think of the clarity or confusion you have in your dreams – that is an example of what happens without the delay effect in place.

In other dimensions the relationship between cause and effect is more direct. In the astral realm – which is the fifth dimension and where you go when you dream – the relationship between thoughts and consequence is much closer. That means when you think of something it will occur immediately.

When your physical body dies you survive and live on. There is life after death. You are an eternal entity that is not restricted to your physical body.

Just because you leave your physical body when you die doesn't mean that as soon as it happens you will be enlightened. It also doesn't mean that you will instantly go to heaven.

When you die you will be as you are now. As you are now means in relation to your state of consciousness. You will just be without the restriction of your physical body. You will still be confined to a particular frequency dependent entirely on your level of consciousness.

When you leave your physical body, if you are of a low consciousness it means that your vibration is low. You will find yourself in the lower realms of the astral plane.

You will find other beings that have a low level of consciousness. A low level of consciousness may be represented by actions such as theft and murder. A low level of consciousness means lack of control over your physical impulses. Emotional turmoil also keeps your vibration low. Emotional turmoil is what causes you pain. The lower astral realm is fueled by emotional turmoil and is not the best holiday location after life on earth. It will appear to you as if you are having a nightmare.

This is the place that many people call Hell.

If your consciousness is higher you will go to a place of a higher vibration. You will find peace. When you have reached a state of consciousness that does not require you to come back to the physical world then you will be in the place that has commonly been called Heaven.

You continually reinvent yourself in a new physical body. You reappear in a different physical body over and over again. Each time you take on a new personality and circumstances. Your purpose in reappearing is to experience, learn and master the process of your life.

You may continually reappear without making much progress because life is a difficult and slow process to learn. The delay between cause and effect means that it takes a long time for you to 'click' and realize the relationship between what you do today and what happens tomorrow. Sometimes you don't see that what you do or think now has an effect later. This prevents you from learning quickly and you often repeat the same process over and over again.

The purpose of your recreating yourself in the physical is to experience and learn. The learning process enables you to refine your thoughts and clear emotional energy from your being. This in turn raises your vibration and enables you to advance through to higher dimensions. The dimensions that you will move through have a tighter relationship between thought and its effect, creation. They are bound by different laws and as such require you to vibrate at a higher frequency. You are meant to be continually improving during your life and through subsequent lifetimes, but this can be difficult.

Before you are born, the real you – your Higher Self – actually chooses the circumstances to which you are born. You decide who your parents will be, what you will look like and any other features or circumstances that you find yourself in.

You pick your circumstances so that you can learn particular things. You can pick your life competently because your Higher Self is the part of you without ego and is not influenced by the things that influence you whilst you are in your physical body. This means that you are not looking for a life of comfort, fame and wealth. You are looking for experiences to learn from. Later you will learn how to do this.

You, the eternal being, deliberately manifested your physical body for a particular purpose. It is your choice to be who you are today. You have decided the shape and characteristics of your physical body. Having a physical body allows you to experience and learn in a certain way that would not be possible as you really are. Existing physically you are unique, and as such have your own circumstances to contend with.

You also choose these circumstances. There are certain things that you will experience that I cannot. Your body is different to mine and your circumstances are different to mine. What can I learn by being born to my parents that you cannot? What can you learn by being you, in your body, that I cannot? There are things that you have experienced with your inner being that the rest of us can never truly know. Without the challenge of life there would be no forward movement and we would cease to exist. This is the law of duality and you will learn this in detail later.

Your past lives are a signal as to why you are having this life. Your interpretations created emotion. Your actions in a past life reshaped energy and created a wave that karma needs to rebalance. So you built up a past file. This needs to be resolved, and often you will need new circumstances to be able to resolve and further learn. Sometimes the emotions you carry are incredibly strong because they are carried for a long time.

You need to rebalance your karma. Reincarnation or rebirth is really just a balancing of energy. You need to have balanced energy before you can move on. To balance your energy you need to move to the middle ground, away from the extreme poles of duality. Whenever you stray from the middle ground in terms of energy you create karma, which needs to be balanced.

This is like saying you have expended too much energy to the left and now you need to give some to the right. Practically you know when you have gone too far left or right because the pull has emotion with it. When your choices are loaded with emotion your choices are unbalanced with a bias to one of the poles.

You get more than one chance to balance energy. If you cannot create balance during this lifetime then you will have a chance during one of your future lifetimes.

Our Purpose

"The purpose of human life is to serve, and to show compassion and the will to help others."

Albert Schweitzer

One of the first questions to answer is that of why are you actually here. What is the purpose of being alive? This is different to the question what is the purpose of your life?

Your ultimate goal is to rejoin with the all-encompassing energy force that most people call God. Whether you believe in God or not is irrelevant. There is an intelligent energy source that permeates throughout the universe and binds it together. Call it God or whatever you like. I don't care; neither does God.

Ultimately you are here on a path to rejoin with this energy source. You are already a part of it and your mission is to become one with it again. I say again because originally that's where you started.

You rejoin with the energy source very simply by refining your energy and increasing your vibration. Over time this enables you to move through the different dimensions and ultimately rejoin with the source that is God.

Before you need to attend to this, you first have to master the physical dimension that you are now operating in. You are born onto the earth for a reason. You are given physical circumstances so that you can do something physical in them. This may just be a matter of survival or the task at hand may be your enlightenment. Everyone is different. Enlightenment is the ability to listen to your soul and allow its light to shine through you. There are different degrees of enlightenment, and when you are fully enlightened you don't need your physical body any more – you will be able to move to a higher dimension.

Self-improvement is the way through the physical dimension.

Yes, it's really simple. Through self-improvement you refine the energy that is you. This heightens your vibration and it allows you to eventually move through the physical realm. You improve yourself by living, experiencing and learning from your experience.

Self-improvement is the purpose of your life. Rejoining with the source is the purpose of life. You will learn more about the meaning of life further on in this text.

For self-improvement to take place there must be change.

Your Attitude Matters

"Nothing can stop the man with the right mental attitude from achieving his goal; nothing on earth can help the man with the wrong mental attitude."

Thomas Jefferson

Attitude is a leaning in one direction relative to a goal. In this case the goal would be to learn. Attitude is not good and it's not bad. It just is.

When you hear someone use the term "good attitude" it just means leaning towards whatever you are talking about. You either have an attitude for or against something. It is the direction your mind leans toward. The only way to learn is to have a positive attitude, and positive means leaning towards what you are going to learn. Without a positive attitude you can't achieve anything and you won't be able to learn.

This leaning towards a certain direction helps you move in that direction. Observe what happens if you wish to slide a heavy object across the room. You lean towards it. If you lean in the opposite way, away from the object, it is nearly impossible to move. If you wish to improve your performance and move the object faster or move a heavier object you need to lean further forward.

Having a negative attitude is like trying to go north when you are moving south.

Another person's attitude affects yours if you let it. You stop it affecting you by deciding that it will not affect you. Formally making a decision requires you to first be aware of what is occurring and has the effect of strengthening you against negative input.

It's almost impossible not to have an attitude. You create your attitude in your mind even if you are unaware of it. It's called your opinion. You unconsciously form an opinion once you are subjected to information. You have the power to change it.

Your attitude can effect positive change in your life.

To get what you want implies that you don't have it now or today. In order to get it, you have to change something in a positive way.

Everything changes. The weather changes daily and the seasons change throughout the year. The leaders of your community change periodically and technology changes rapidly. You and your body change over time. Your childhood disappears and you become an adult. Your feelings change from moment to moment, and even if you remain in the same job for a lifetime you will notice that the nature of that job changes.

There is nothing that remains a constant, and there is a cliché that says, "The only constant is change."

Rather than fight and resist change, go with it and embrace change because it is inevitable. Change the way you want or you will change in a way you don't want. For instance, I sometimes see older people who resist modern technology. They become redundant in the work place. You think that by not changing things remain the same. They don't; in this example you are changed relative to the new world that you live in.

Change is good or bad depending on your perspective. The weather changes from a beautiful and warm summer to a bitterly cold winter. Terrible if you love water skiing but perhaps you have been waiting all year to go snow skiing.

Everything changes and things are never the same. If they stayed the same then they would be indefinable; I mean they would cease to be noticeable and therefore cease to exist.

Let's use the weather as an example. If it was sunny everyday and it was 22 degrees everyday, forever, then there would be no weather. We simply wouldn't have any knowledge about it because it never changes.

Contrast happens because of change. Without change there would be no contrast. Without contrast things cease to exist.

Without good there would be no evil; without black, there would be no white. Change and contrast is not always so obvious. Look in the mirror and try to discern how many more wrinkles you have today compared to yesterday. This is not easy. To make the task simpler, look in the mirror and compare your face with a photograph taken twenty years before. The difference in temperature between 22 degrees and 23 degrees is not discernable without a thermometer.

Change is your learning tool. Change allows you to experience. Change allows you to learn about the entire range of possibilities that are available in this physical existence. Once you have knowledge of the extremes you are able to find peace at the balance point between them. You gain knowledge as you move between the extremes of change.

Everything is moving. This means that change is inevitable – there is nothing you can do about it. You sometimes miss the fact that everything is moving in the same way we can't see that the earth is round and that the planet is actually spinning. It's because of the magnitude of the cycles of change that are involved.

You get 'stuck' because change can be frightening so you don't let go of things. The trick is to ride the wave of experience and then learn to let go. You are attracted to something; you experience it and then you have to let go otherwise the energy gets stale. If you like chocolate cake and you start to eat and it brings you pleasure, after a while you need to change and stop eating otherwise it will bring you displeasure from eating too much. You have to let go. A cycle is now complete. You can re-experience the cake again but if you go through too many cycles of eating cake this becomes a cycle of too much of the wrong food. You become uncomfortable by not changing. You can apply similar examples to television, reading your favorite book, your work or career – in fact anything at all.

In order for you to change, you must first understand what it is that you need to change. To understand you have to study and then practice.

Mastering Your Life – Key to Success

Everything comes from inner change. You often look to the outside world for solutions like a different set of circumstances, believing that this will change the way you feel or bring you happiness. The only way to find a true solution is internally. In fact, the answers are contained within you.

The key of life is contained within you. You are a complex receiver and transmitter of energy. Energy is that which is happening around you. In order to be able to turn the key and have whatever you want you need to understand how you work.

There are several things that you need to do to master life in this physical dimension. Once you have achieved them you move on to another realm.

There is no rule that says you must do it in this lifetime. However, the closer you get to mastery the easier your physical existence gets. Everyone feels a pull towards enlightenment eventually. That doesn't mean you will just miraculously wake one day and be enlightened. It means that you will feel a pull and start looking for the answers. Eventually you will realize that the solution is in the doing. It's all about action.

There are four things that you have to do to master life:

1. You need to increase your consciousness.

   That means allowing the divine spark that is found in you to shine through.

2. You need to learn to be a creator with your thoughts.

   Creating with your thoughts means turning thoughts to substance. It means you have to express yourself.

3. You need to eliminate emotional ties.

   Emotional ties are what prevent you from increasing your consciousness. Emotions stop you seeing clearly.

4. You have to look after your physical vehicle.

Without your physical body it is impossible to do any of the above. If you are unhealthy you are hampered in your progress.

These four points are the purpose of you living life.

Enlightenment

"A life is either all spiritual or not spiritual at all. No man can serve two masters. Your life is shaped by the end you live for. You are made in the image of what you desire."

Thomas Merton

All of these things lead to what is called enlightenment.

Enlightenment is an ideal state of being that can be achieved via an ongoing process. It is the process of allowing more light, or the maximum amount of consciousness, to shine through your physical being.

Some people know this process as the search for the Holy Grail. You do not find enlightenment. It is achieved by removing its obstacles. These obstacles are inside of you and are created by your mind.

Let me explain it another way. When you are enlightened you are liberated from the physical world. Liberated from the physical world doesn't mean you suddenly disappear and have no need for a physical body. Liberation is the freedom to see beyond your day-to-day existence and the emotions that go with it.

Here is what it means to be enlightened:

1. You have the ability to witness your thought process.

Your thoughts create your future physical reality. You currently identify with your thoughts. You live your life inside your thought processes and don't realize that your thoughts are separate to you. The vast majority of your thinking is conducted without you being aware of what is being thought. You ride these thoughts to fruition, often to your detriment. When you are enlightened, you free yourself from being swept up in your thinking process and therefore liberate yourself from any result that is not your choice.

2. You are free from suffering.

You currently suffer every time you wrestle with emotion, argue about something or agonize over a decision. Sometimes this is short-lived and mild, and at other times it is extremely painful and remains with you for a long period of time. When you are free from suffering you will however still say something colorful when you stub your toe!

3. You are free of desire.

Desire means you are unsatisfied, and in this state your wants are driven by emotion. Without desire you can still have, but your want is much closer to a preference. When you experience this you will understand freedom from the material world. This doesn't mean you can't have or pursue chocolate cake. It just means you don't lust after it and you are unaffected if you don't get it.

4. You can see the truth.

The truth is the way that the world really is. Being able to see the truth means you see beyond the physical shell of others. You see who they really are. It means you can read between the lines and really hear what others are saying.

Note: Notice how there is nothing said about religion. Notice also how there is no mention of morals and what you can and can't do.

The transfer of energy – both positive and negative – occurs between all people who connect in any way, shape or form. When you are enlightened your consciousness is higher than the majority of people you come into contact with. That means you have the ability to affect other people in a positive way with your energy. I am doing it now through the words of this book, but there is a much simpler way. You can do it just by sitting near others. Your heightened consciousness will impact on others and they will benefit from the passive transfer of energy that occurs.

Consciousness

Your consciousness is the real you. It is the divine spark in you. Some people know this by the following ters: m

1. Your Higher Self.

2. A higher intelligence.

3. Your Over Soul.

4. Your Super Conscious mind.

5. Your Creative Subconscious mind.

6. The Holy Spirit.

7. The Collective Consciousness.

I am sure there are other terms that are used to describe the same energy. Consciousness is the amount of your Higher Self, your true intelligence, that shines through.

When you live with an increased consciousness you have freedom from:

1. An emotional and reactive state of being.

2. An intellectual state of being, which is a calculating mind that is based on logic alone.

Both of these states are governed by self-interest. Self-interest is the incorrect state to work from because it blocks the flow of energy around you and therefore destroys the quality of your life. Remember we are all one. When you act as if you are separate you block the flow of energy.

Consciousness is being aware and acting without the bias of the intellect and emotions. It is the ability to act from a position of love. When you increase your consciousness you are able to interpret what happens around you, clearly.

When you allow your consciousness to shine through you will see beyond your immediate circumstances. You will see more. This is what's meant in the Bible when Jesus performs a miracle and gives a blind man sight. You will have the ability to let go of hate and other negative emotions and embrace a better state of being. This higher state of being allows you to escape the grip of the material world.

You activate and you increase your consciousness by being aware.

When you are being aware it means you are present and in the 'now' state. Being present allows you to be aware. The contrasting state is to be in a daydream, which you may spend a good majority of your life in. The part of you that is aware and present is your consciousness.

You need to be conscious of what is happening to you internally and externally to be aware. Most people move through the day in one of two states:

1. You are unaware of what is physically happening around you because you are focused internally. You may not have noticed the driver of the car next to you. You are unaware of the bird chirping in the background or the noise of the truck driving past. You may have experienced driving along the freeway daydreaming and unconsciously following the car in front of you only to wake up later at your destination or many kilometers down the road. You may be stressed and anxious about a situation because your thoughts are focused on an unlikely but negative future outcome.

   To overcome this temporary state you need to stop and push yourself outward. You do this with your consciousness.

2. You are unaware of what is happening internally because you are focused externally. You may not have noticed that you are feeling the emotion of guilt or fear because you are running late to work and your mind is on the traffic.

To overcome this temporary state you need to use your consciousness to pull yourself inward.

To be aware and to live in awareness you need to observe your external world and your internal world simultaneously.

To look at your external world with your senses means to monitor your five senses. Look at the color of the ingredients as you make your lunch. Feel the texture as you touch them. Hear the noise you make as you work, and smell the finished product as you taste it. Live in the present moment and experience what's happening. The contrasting state is daydreaming about what someone said yesterday and missing out on the experience of what you are doing now. In this daydream world you can live your whole life and miss out on what happens.

Monitor your internal world. Look at how you feel. You may experience strange sensations in your mid-section when your boss tells you to do something. You will feel the tension in your shoulders or the tightness in your face if you direct your attention to that area. Perhaps you feel anger when you watch the evening news. You might be thinking about something that happened throughout the day. Awareness allows you to see what is happening in your internal world.

Stop reading and do the following exercise.

Exercise 1 – Being Present

Practice the state of being present.

You do this by continually waking to the fact that you have slipped into a daydream about the past or future. When you wake and catch this moment, use your senses to be aware of what's going on in your world both internally and externally. Do NOT get lost in thinking about your senses. The trick here is to USE your senses.

Do this continually as many times in the day as you can. Keep count. Each time you wake yourself after slipping back into a daydream counts as one. If you lose count during the day you start the count again at one.

Aim for 30 to 120 repetitions per day. If you are getting less than 30 you need to pay more attention to this exercise. Do this for seven days before reading on

Exercise 2 – Awareness Exercise

Get a pencil and paper.

Be still and observe what is happening around you. What can you pick up with your five senses? Write a list of thirty things.

Observe your internal world. What are you thinking and how and what do you feel? Write it down, make a list.

You may be unaware of what's happening to you because you are unconscious to it. You may be working on autopilot and going through the motions of experiencing your life. It is your mind that takes you away from what you are doing now. What you are doing now is what you need to experience. The constant chatter in your mind is what blocks your experience of now.

You continually think about the past or the future. This means that you are living your life in your thoughts of the past and the future.

The past is gone and doesn't exist anymore. Stop for a moment and take a handful of the past and hold it up. You can't do it. It doesn't exist. The same applies to thoughts about the future. The future is not yet happening. You need to focus on now.

Awareness is a balanced state in which you can observe what's happening around you and what's happening to you. This state is also called being present. Your consciousness is what is allowed through when you are in awareness. Your consciousness is the pure you.

There are signals that indicate you are in a state of awareness and fully conscious. By fully conscious I don't mean that you have allowed the maximum amount of consciousness that is possible to enter your physical being. I mean to be as aware and conscious as is possible now.

1. You will experience clarity and depth of vision.

2. You will see and experience things in greater detail.

3. You will have unexplainable feelings of happiness or joy.

4. Time seems to disappear. It's like the feeling you have doing something you absolutely love.

One of the easiest ways to begin seeking awareness is to create anchor points throughout the day. Split your day into three sections. Then, three times per day, stop, close your eyes and breathe in deeply. Open your eyes and become aware.

When you have built a habit from this, split each section of your day into two and you will now have five anchor points, and so on. Aim to have an anchor point every hour. Then expand the length of time that you are aware at each anchor point. Instead of a few seconds, extend the time. Eventually your new state of being aware will dominate your day.

This is something that requires continual practice.

Conclusion

It's been an honorable journey serving you and providing you with what's necessary for you to grow and expand beyond your current limits and challenges. Take action and live the life you truly deserve, it's simple, it's not easy changing your life, it takes dedication, if you're meant to succeed, you will, because the mind translates your values and standards into a reality. Knowing who you truly are, is extremely important, first you **have to** know yourself and then you can experience everything The World can offer to the fullest!

Huge Thank You and Words of Gratitude!

First and foremost, Thank You for downloading this book. At the end of the day I'm **extremely** grateful for **every** download and **every** purchase. It really makes me smile and motivates me. I wish that every person would put their best forward for the human race. I wish you unlimited mental strength and discipline to achieve your goals and dreams.

Together we can make the difference.

If you found the information useful I would be extremely grateful if you could write a short Amazon review. It really does make the difference and I personally read every review and take notes. I want to improve my books, so that I can provide more value to other people. I know that my future books will give you the best experience possible.

Your Free Gift

If You so desire you can listen to the book...
Just as promised – free audio version of this book for my lovely readers !

Please visit the link below

http://eepurl.com/btAtzn

Copyright

Printed in Great Britain
by Amazon